MAZE

Vol 6

Ages 4-6

FOR KIDS

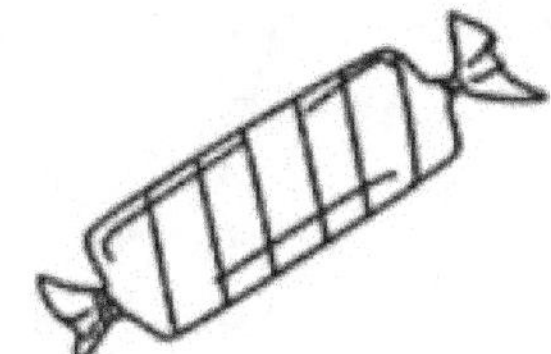

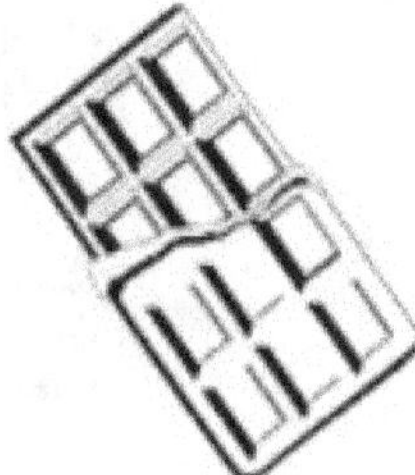

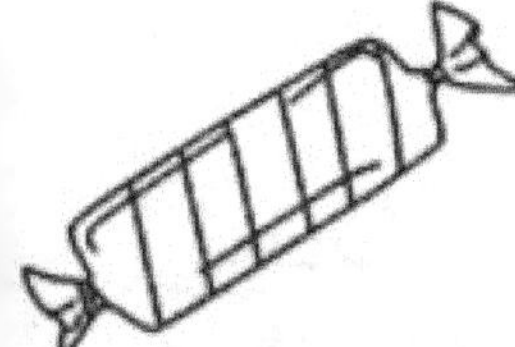

MAZE BOOK

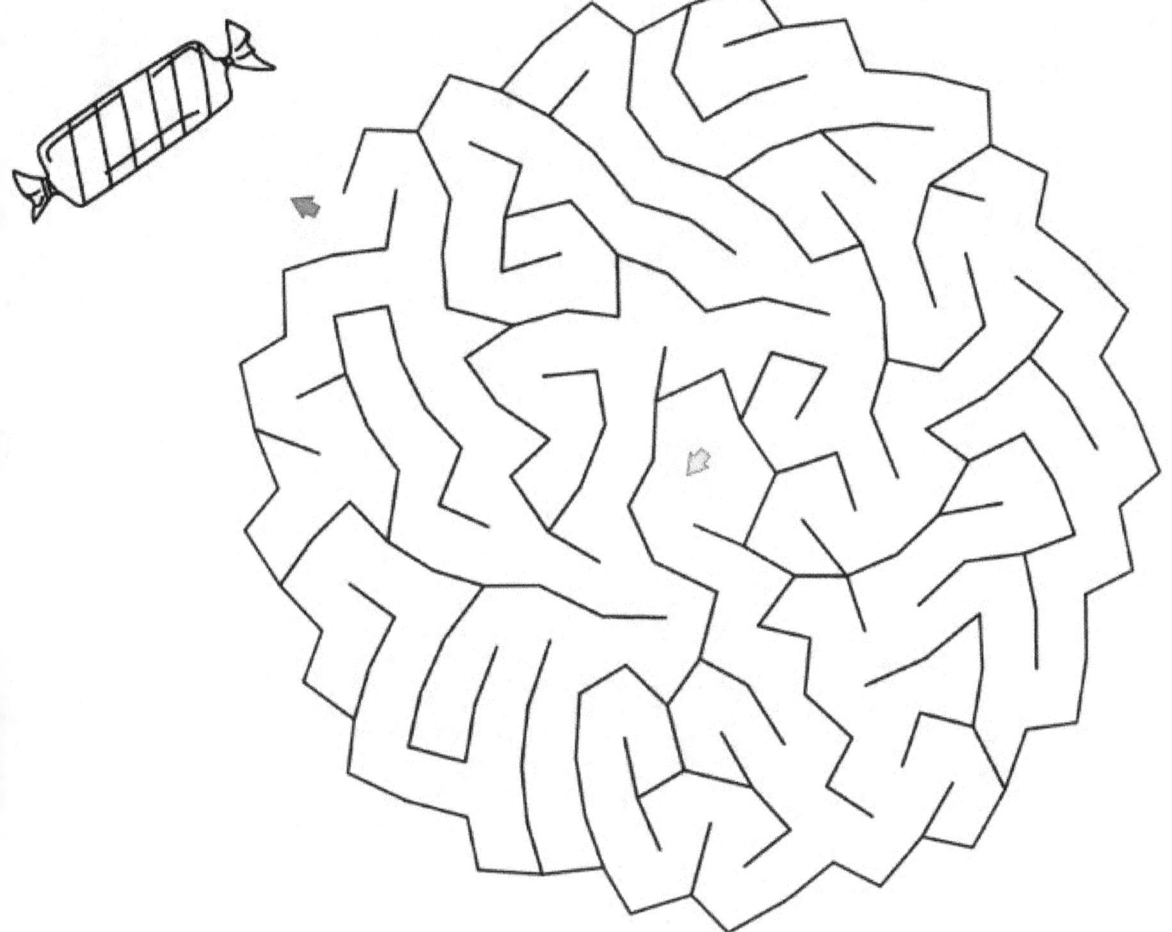

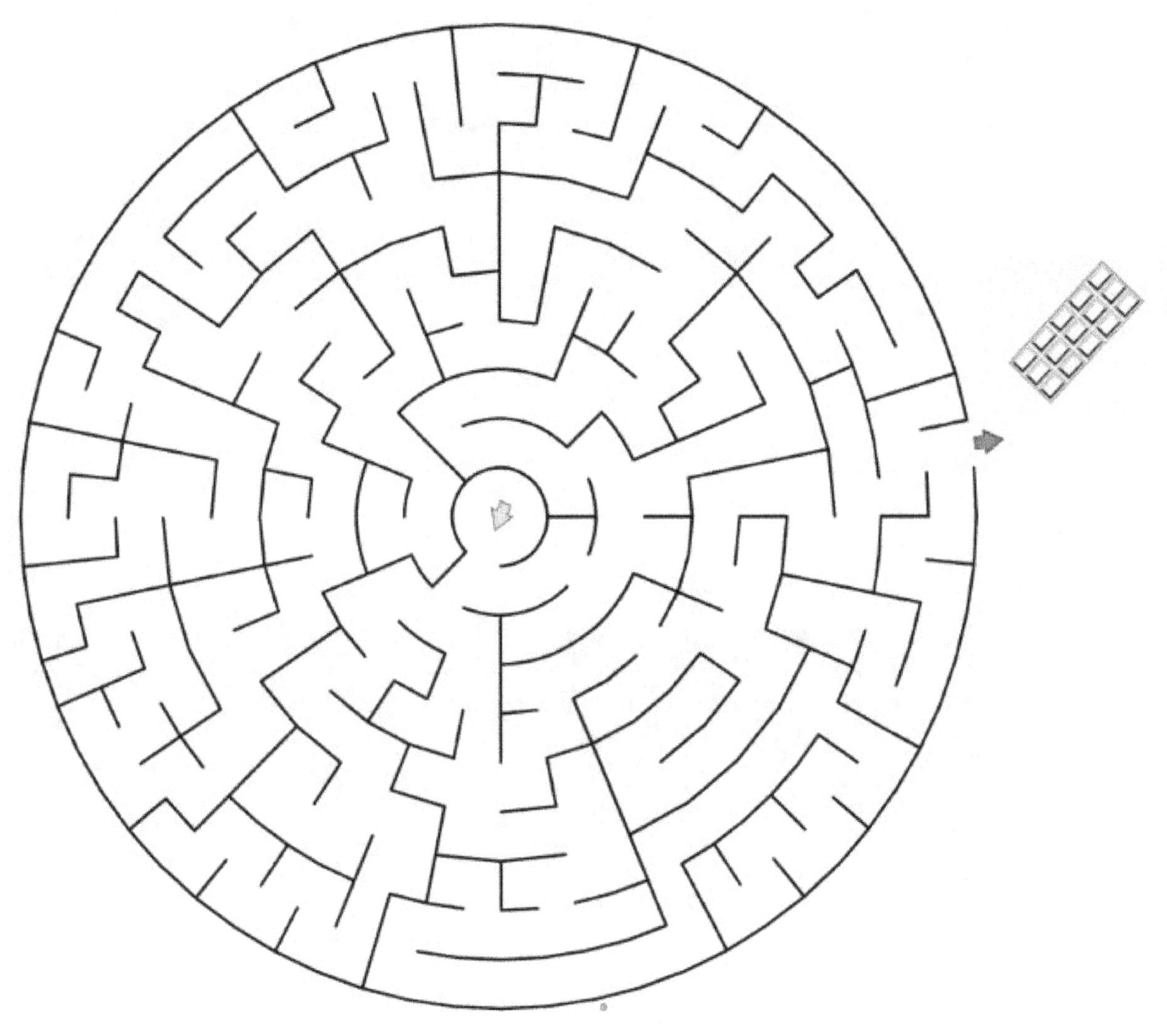

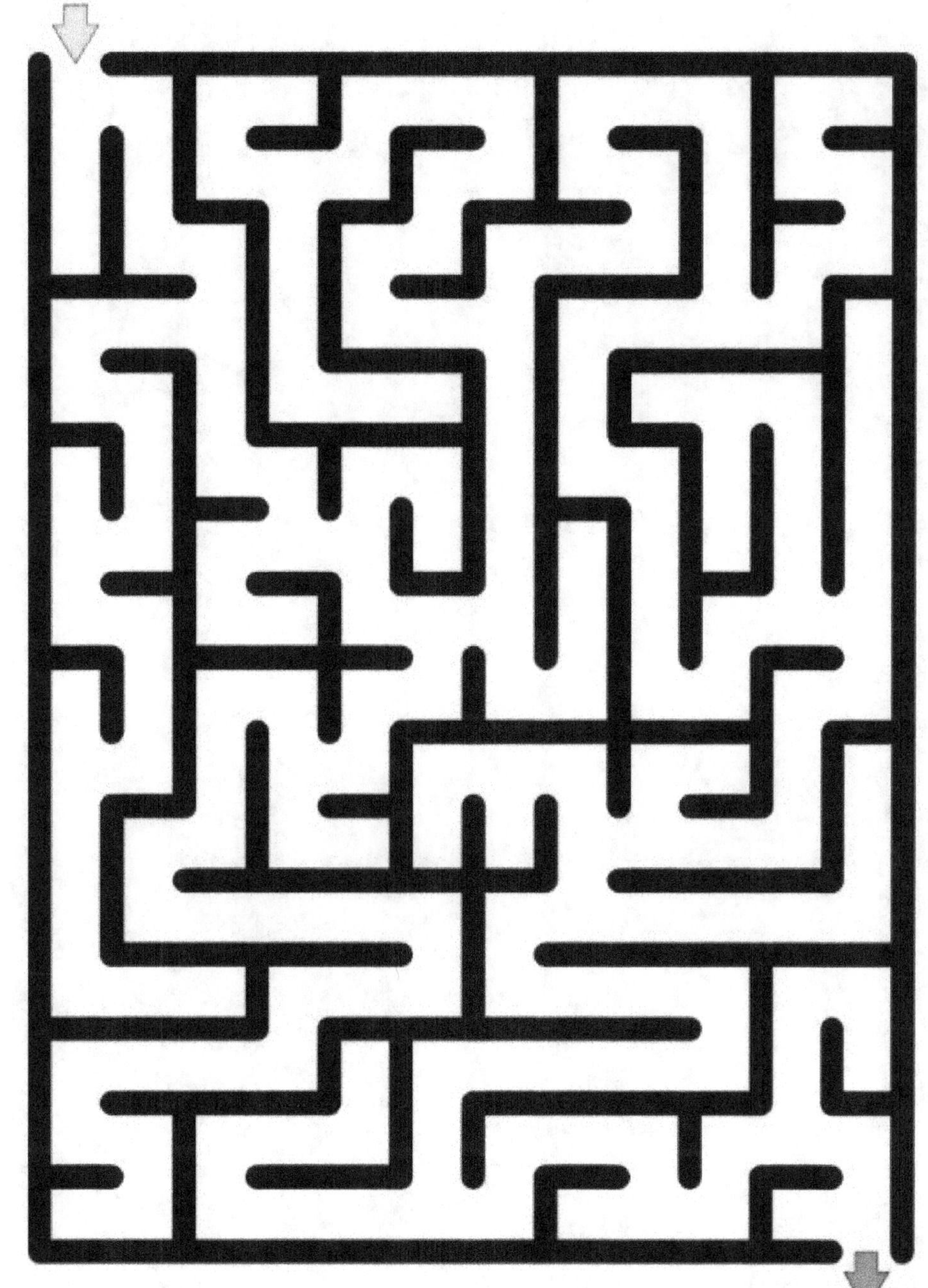

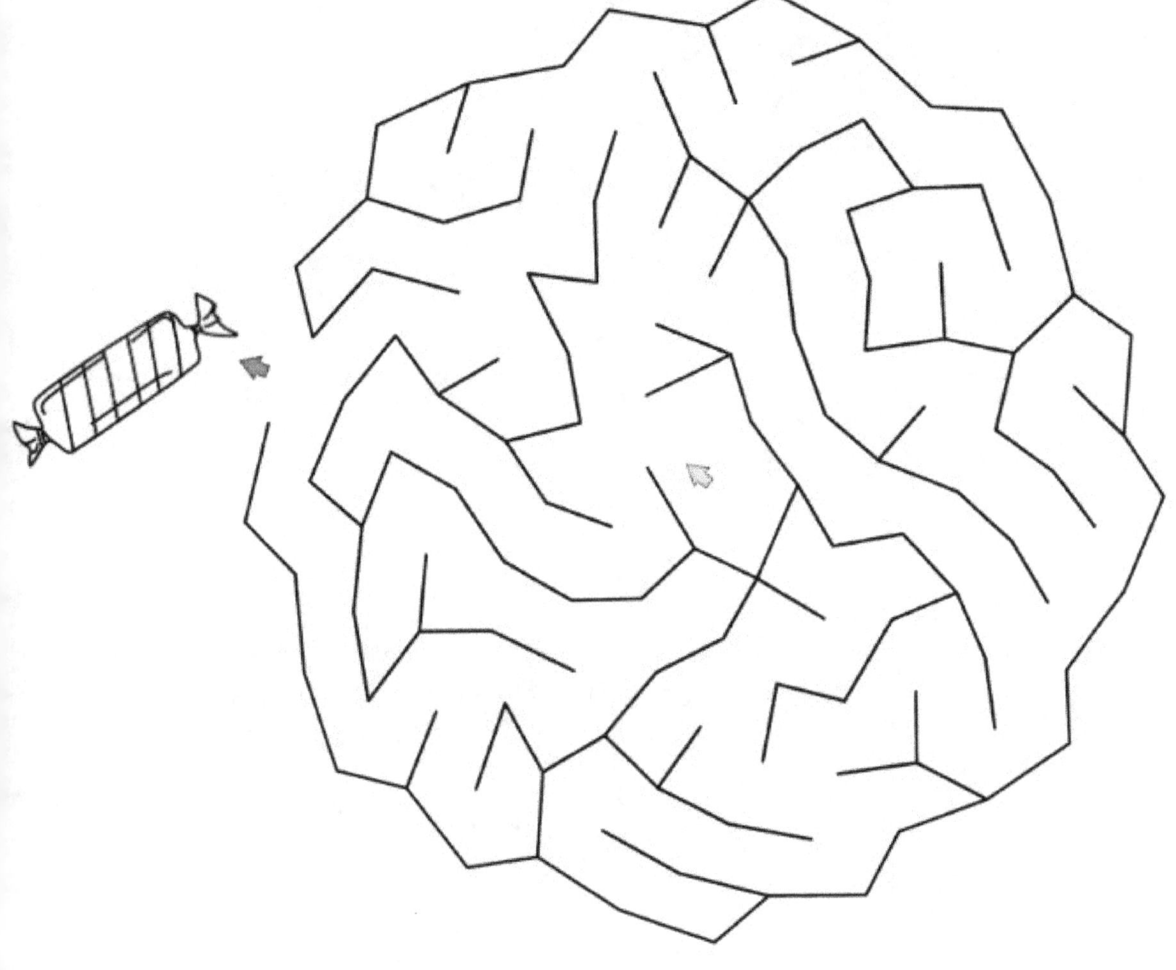

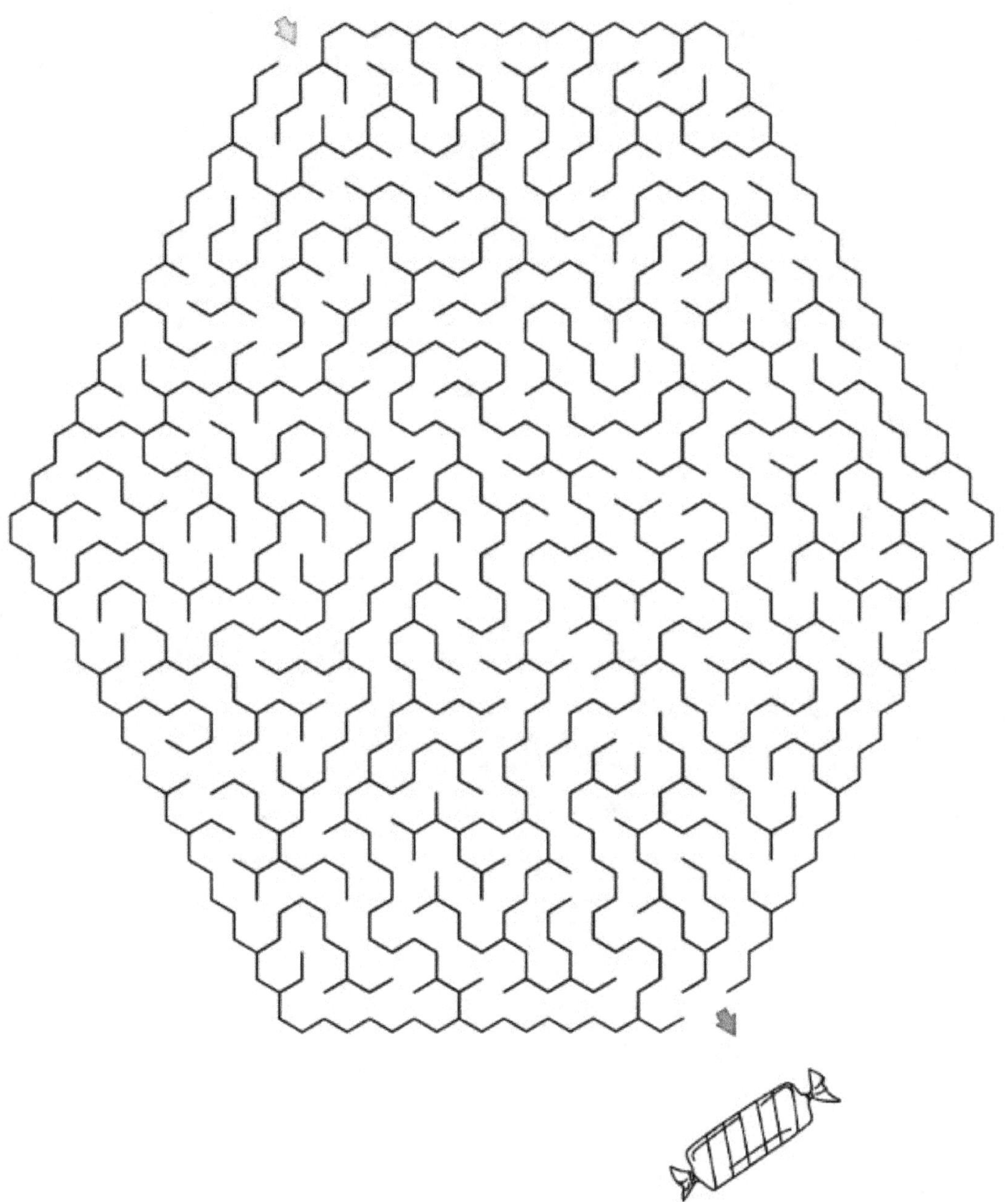

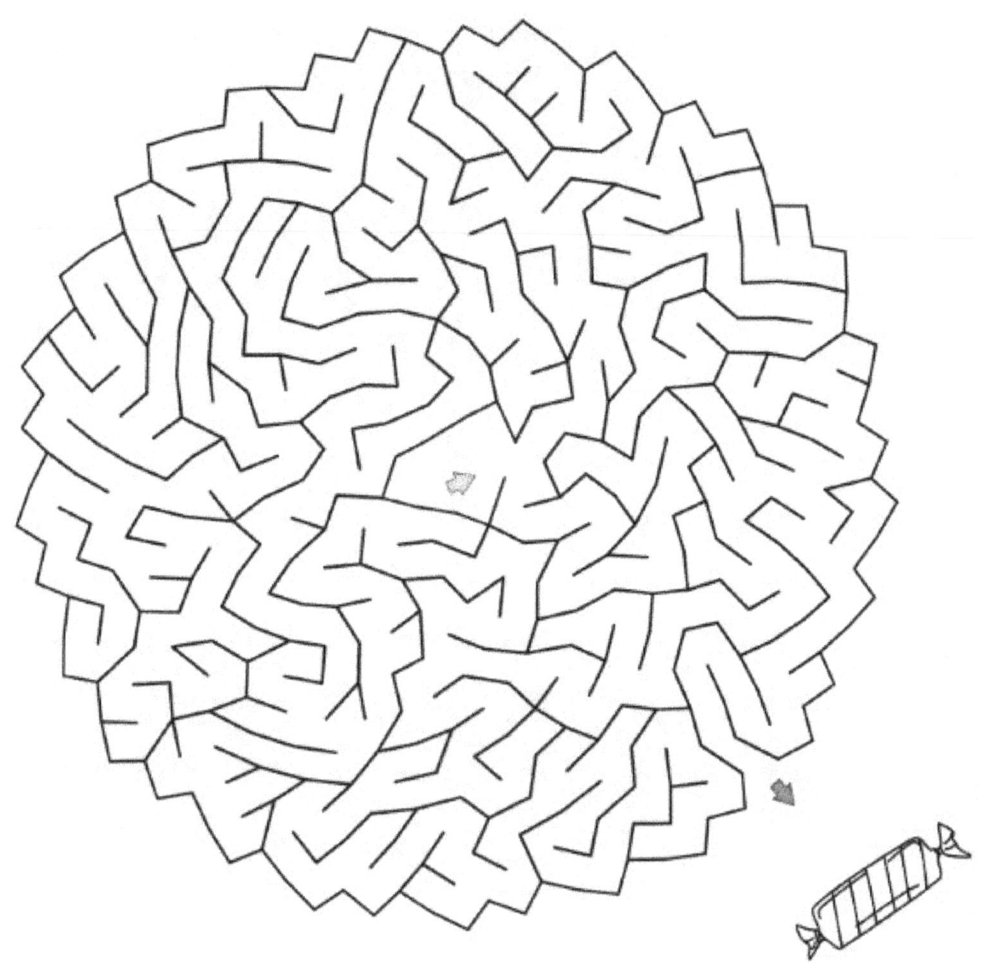

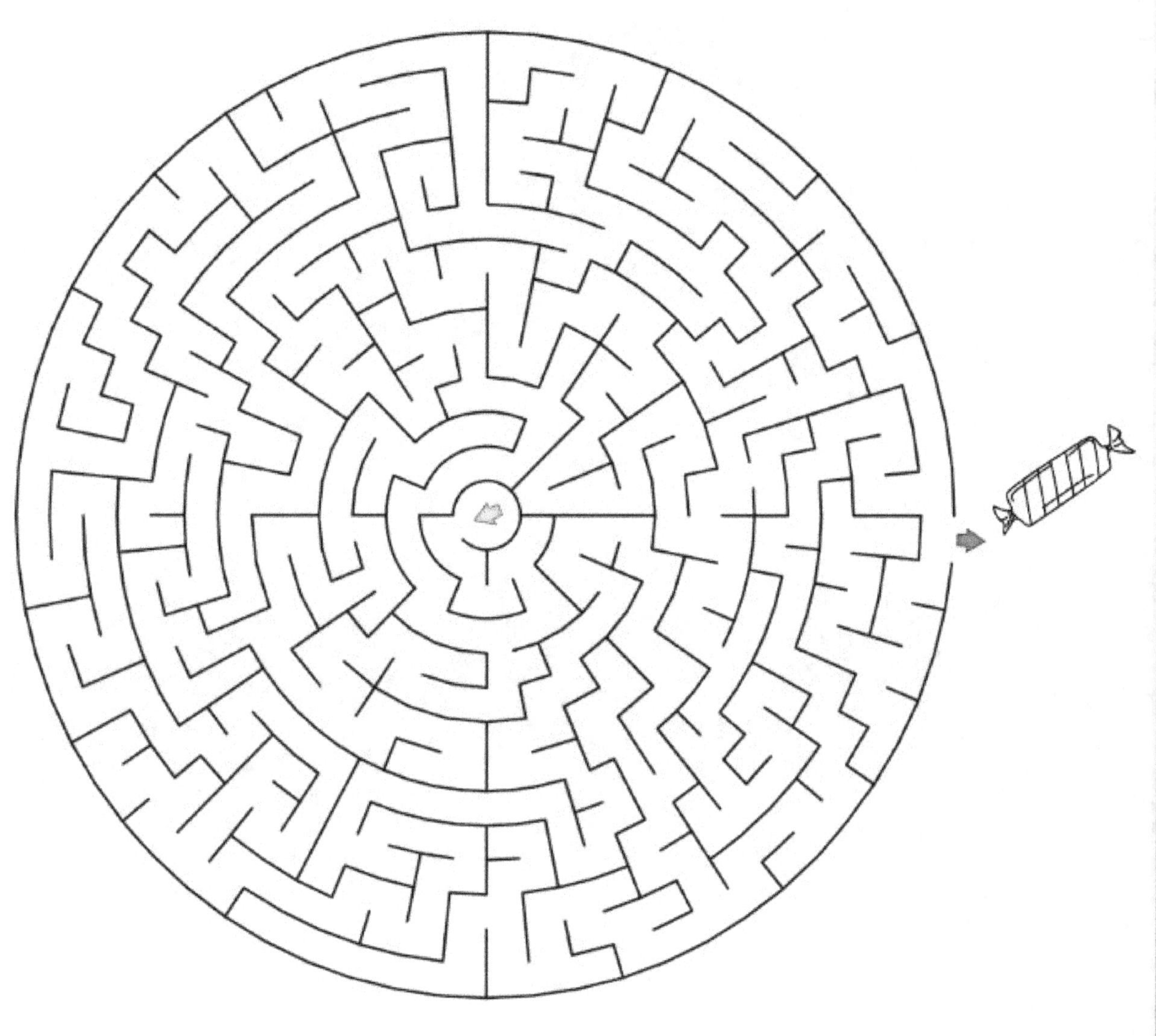

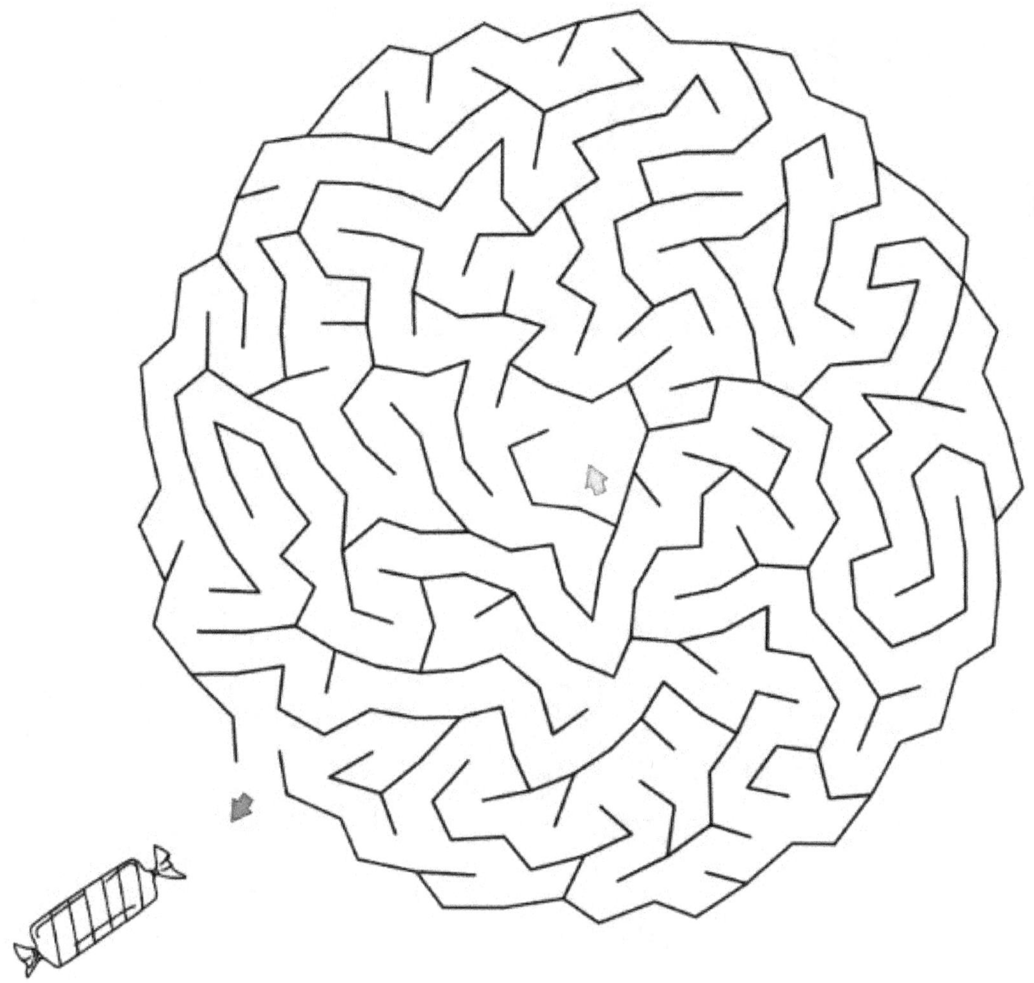

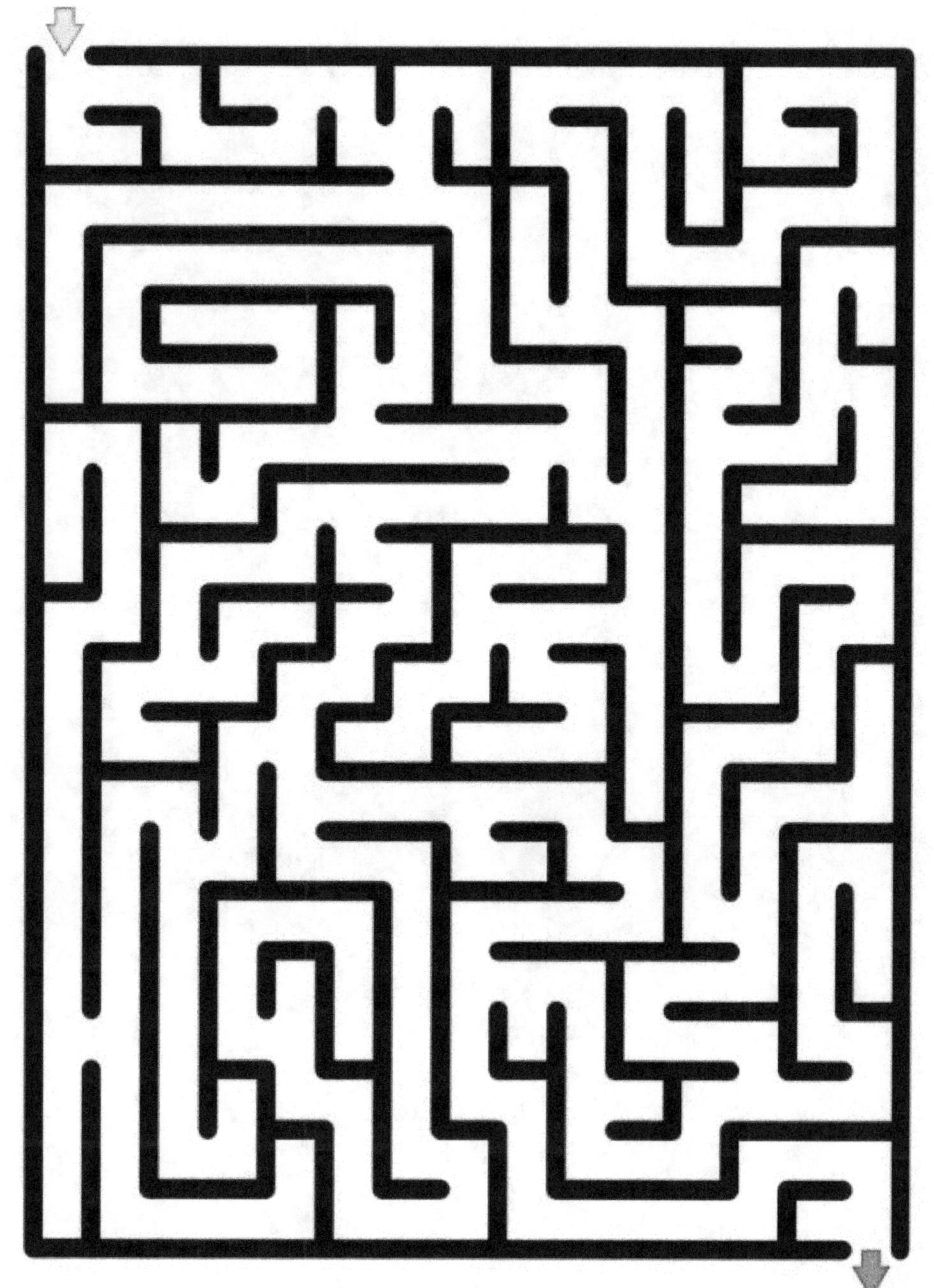

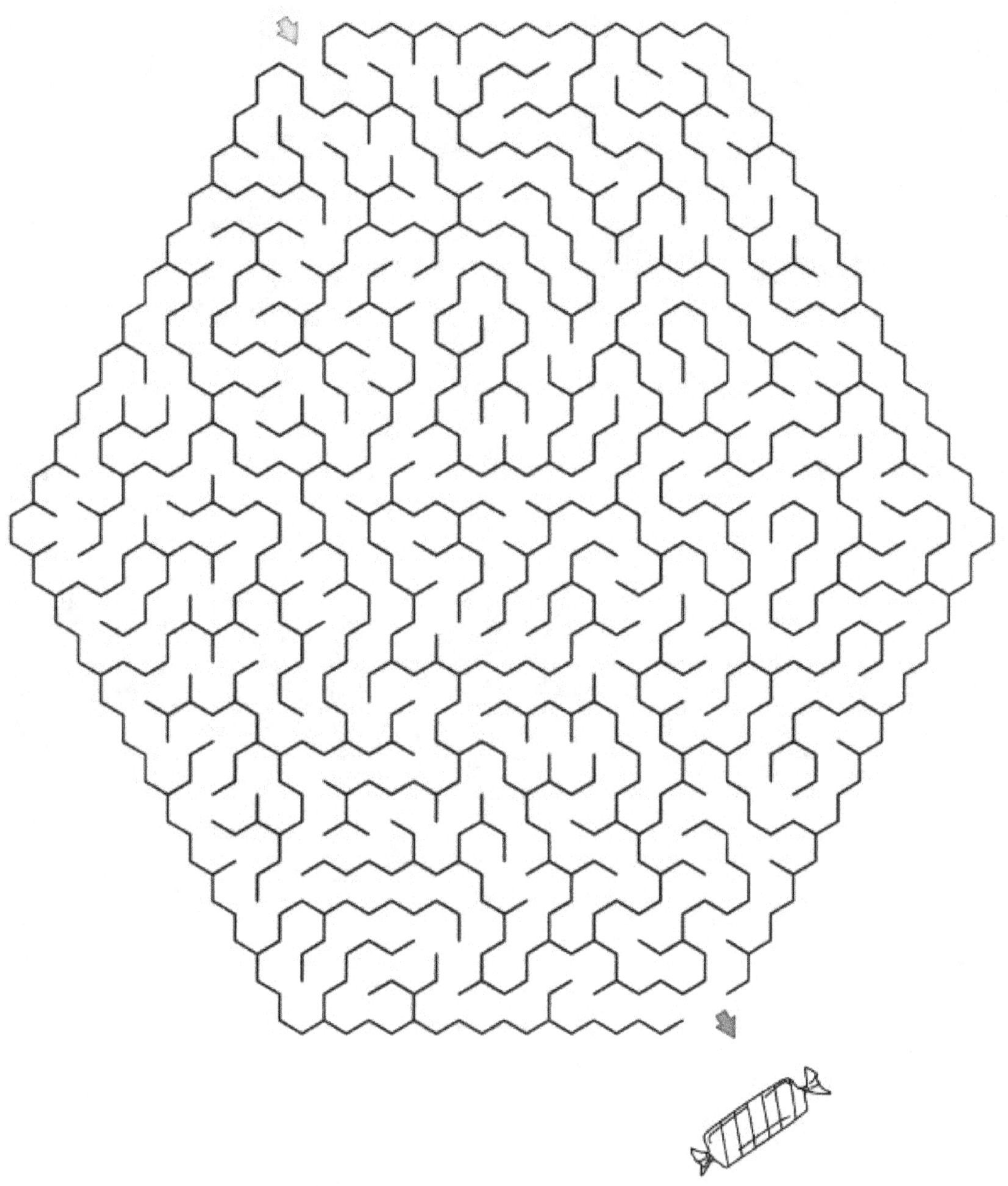

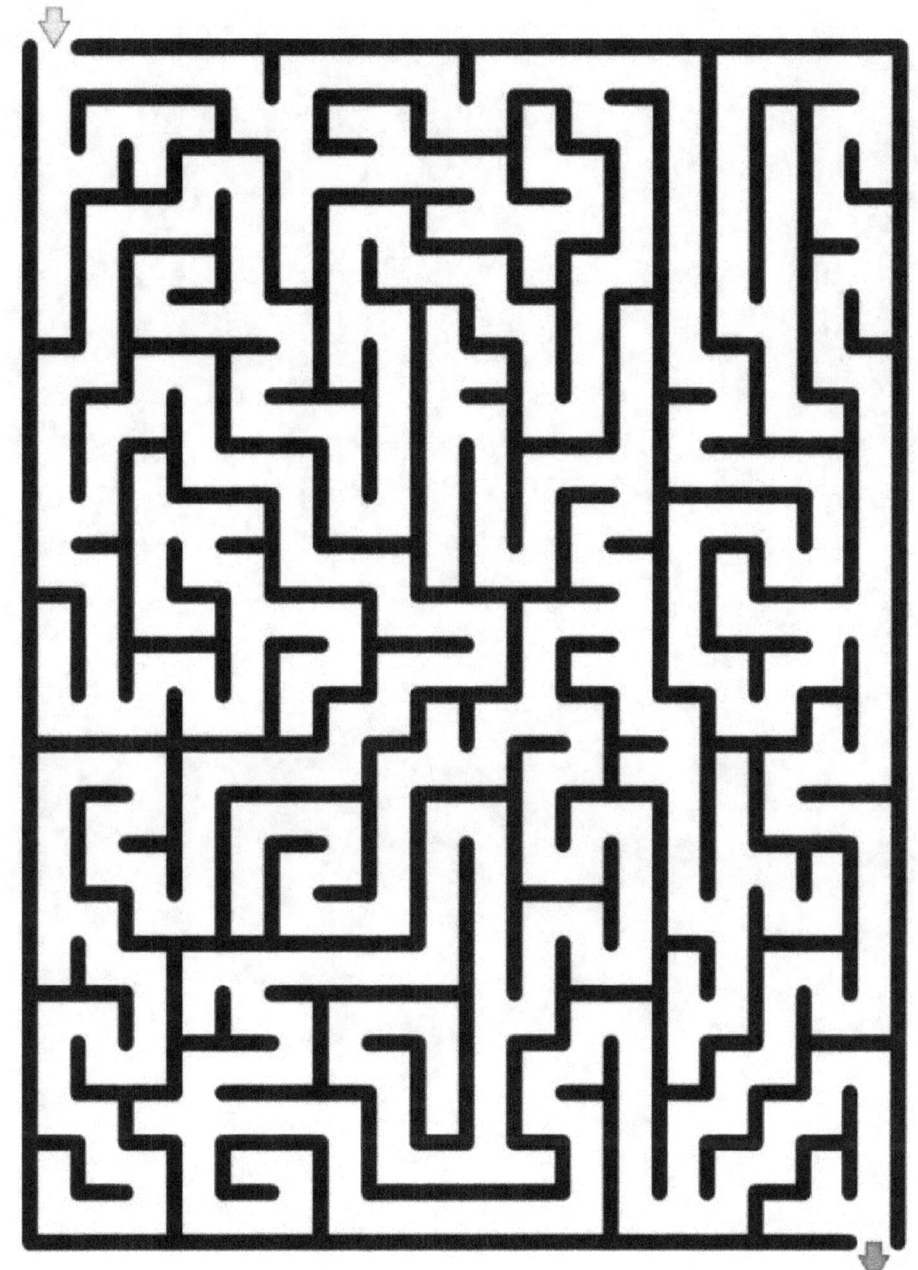

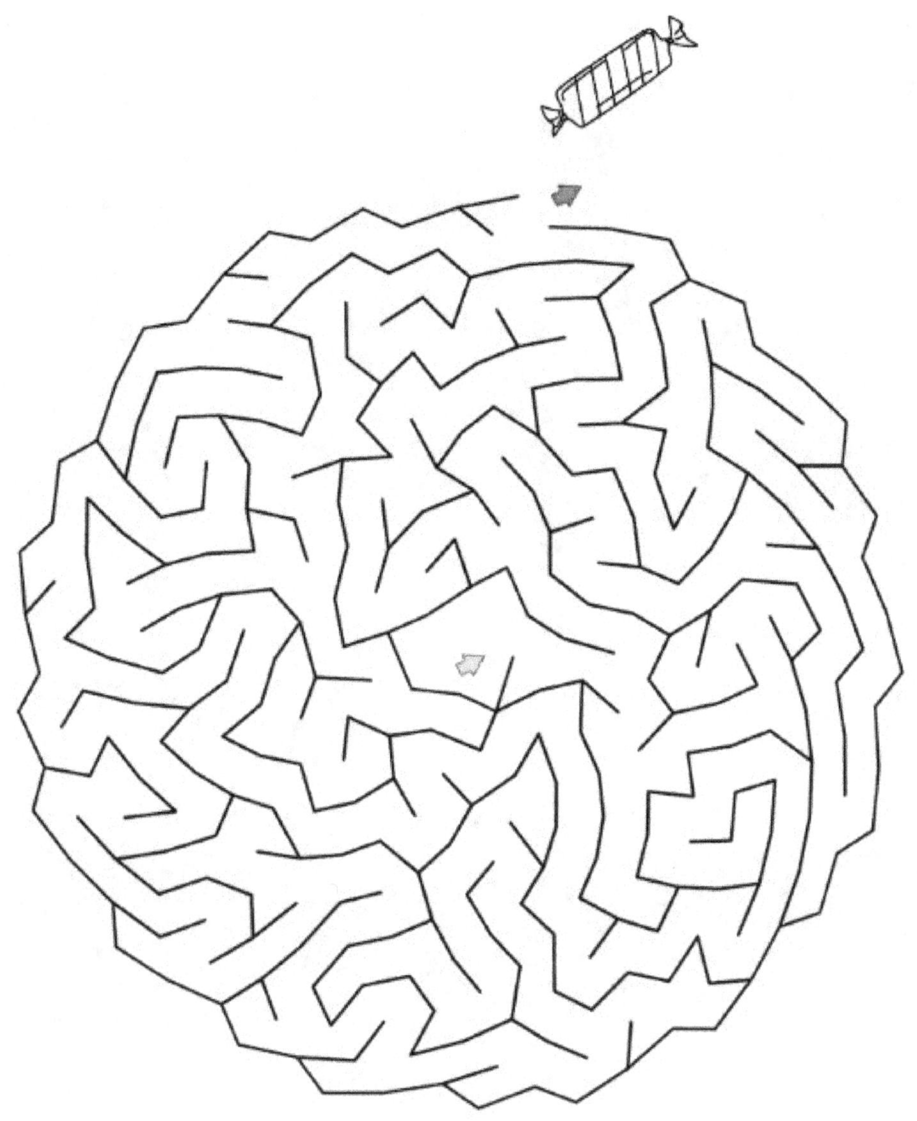

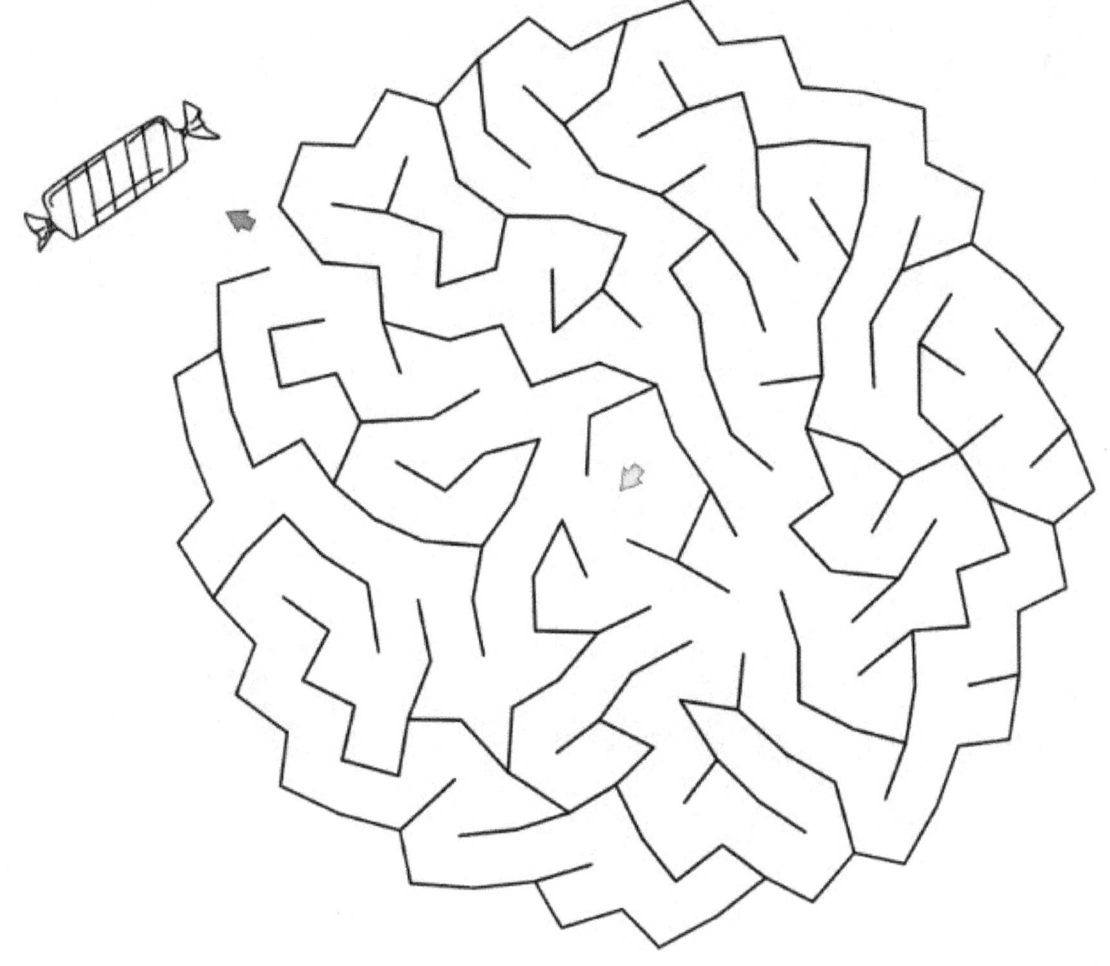

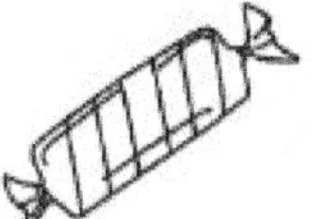

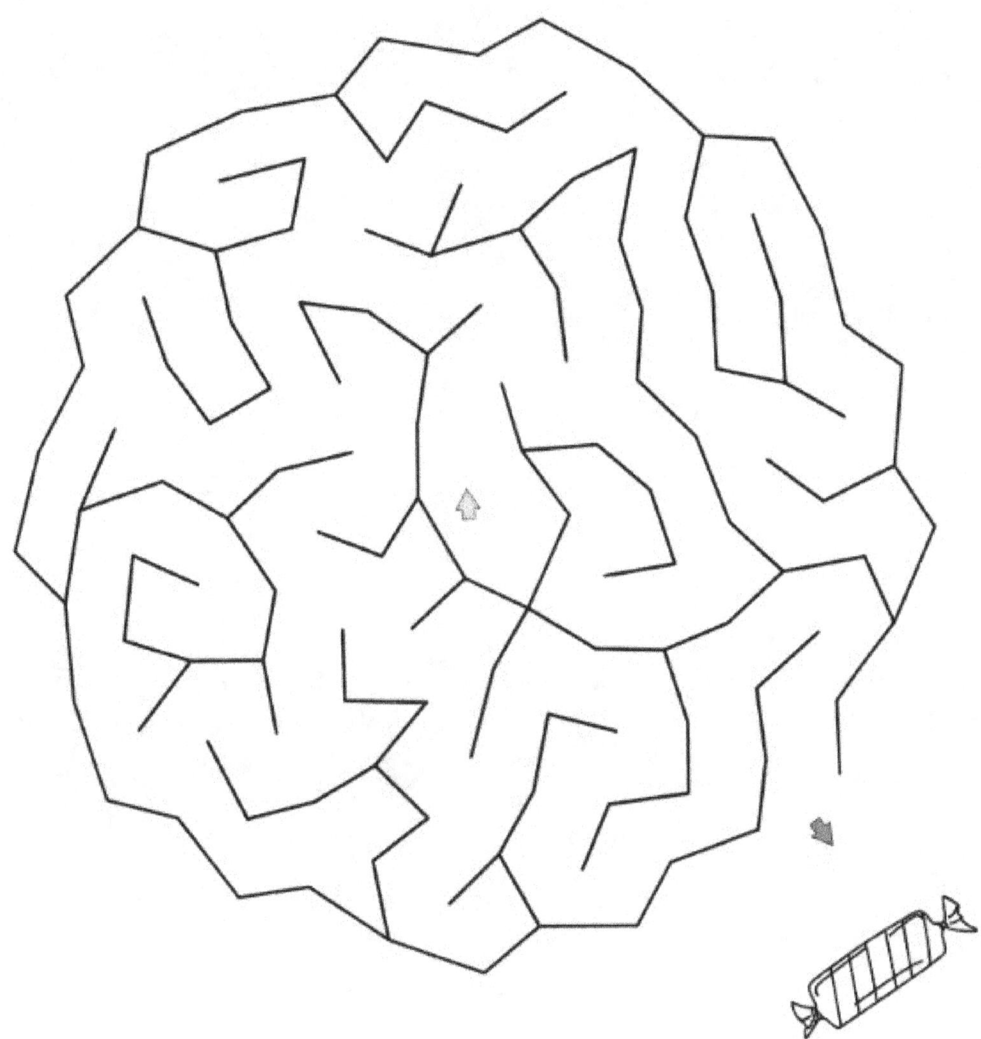